Dream Catcher

A NIGHTTIME JOURNAL

CHRONICLE BOOKS

SAN FRANCISCO

Printed in Singapore.

Library of Congress Cataloging-in-Publication Data available
ISBN 0-8118-0754-1

Editing and design: Big Fish Books
Composition: Jennifer Petersen, Big Fish Books

Distributed in Canada by Raincoast Books,
8680 Cambie Street, Vancouver, B.C. V6P 6M9

10 9 8 7 6 5 4

Chronicle Books
275 Fifth Street
San Francisco, CA 94103

DREAMCATCHER is a journal that allows you to record your *nighttime* thoughts—your dreams. Each page is designed to record one night's dream or dreams. If you have trouble describing an image, the margins can be used for sketches.

DREAMCATCHER should be kept next to your bed each night and dreams should be jotted down as soon as you awake. Don't be afraid to record any dream—even if it's fragmented or scattered. You may find it makes more sense later. Finally, be sure to record the date and time of your dream. This can help you discover the patterns and rhythms of your nighttime thoughts.

D a t e

T i m e

Learn from
your dreams
what you
lack.
—W.H. AUDEN

Date

Time

Date

Time

Date

Time

D a t e

T i m e

I have dreamed
in my life,
dreams that
have stayed
with me ever
after, and
changed my
ideas; they
have gone
through and
through me,
like wine
through water,
and altered
the colour of
my mind.
—EMILY BRONTË

Date

Time

Date

Time

Date

Time

Date

Time

D a t e

_____

T i m e

_____

...the dreamer
and his dream
are the same...
the powers
personified in a
dream are
those that move
the world.
—JOSEPH
CAMPBELL

Date

Time

Date

Time

Date

Time

Date

Time

If we think of
the dream as a
work of
fiction—and I
think it is—
it may be that
we continue to
spin tales when
we wake and
later when we
recount them.

—JORGE LUIS
BORGES

Date

_____

Time

_____

Date

Time

Date
_____

Time
_____

D a t e

T i m e

A dream is
a little hidden
door in the
innermost
and most secret
recesses of the
soul, opening
into that cosmic
night which
was psyche
long before
there was
any ego-
consciousness.
—CARL JUNG

Date

_____

Time

_____

Date

Time

Date

_____

Time

_____

Date
_____

Time
_____

Date

_____

Time

_____

Two gates for
ghostly dreams
there are:
one gateway
of honest horn,
and one of ivory.
Issuing by the
ivory gates are
dreams of
glimmering
illusion,
fantasies, but
those that come
through solid
polished horn,
may be born out,
if mortals only
know them.
—HOMER

Date

_____

Time

_____

Date

Time

Date

_____

Time

_____

D a t e

T i m e

In dreams we
catch glimpses
of a life larger
than our own....
For one fleeting
night a princelier
nature captures
us and we
become as great
as our aspirations.
—HELEN KELLER

Date

_____

Time

_____

Date

Time

Date

Time

Date

Time

I have dreams.
I don't see
what you're
supposed to
do about dreams.
You're always
asleep when
they happen....
Dreams
wouldn't dare
do what they
do to me when
I'm awake.

—MARTIN AMIS

Date

_____

Time

_____

Date

Time

Date

Time

Date

Time

D a t e

_____

T i m e

_____

Let us suppose,
then, that we
are dreaming,
and that
all those
particulars—
namely, the
opening of the
eyes, the motion
of the head, the
forth-putting of
the hands—
are merely
illusions;
and even that
we really
possess neither an
entire body nor
hands such
as we see.
—RENE
DESCARTES

Date

Time

Date

Time

Date

Time

D a t e

T i m e

It is beyond
dispute that I can
fly in dreams.
You too. I add
'in my dreams'
because my
efforts, like yours,
have not
succeeded—
by a sound,
a strangled sigh—
in crossing the
frontier that
separates the two
worlds, only one
of which we
designate,
arbitrarily, as 'real.'
—COLETTE

Date

Time

Date

Time

Date

Time

All dreams of
the soul/
End in
a beautiful
man's or
woman's
body.
—W.B. YEATS

Date
_____

Time
_____

Date

Time

Date

_____

Time

_____

Date

Time

As I live and
am a man,
this is an
unexaggerated
tale—my dreams
become the
substances
of my life.
—S.T.
COLERIDGE

Date

Time

Date

Time

Date

Time

Date

Time

Date

Time

I want to keep
my dreams,
even bad ones,
because without
them, I might
have nothing
all night long.
—JOSEPH HELLER

Date

Time

Date

Time

Date

_____

Time

_____

Date

Time

Date

Time

Dreams! in their
vivid colouring
of life, /
As in that
fleeting, shadowy,
misty strife /
Of semblance
with reality,
which brings /
To the
delirious eye
more lovely
things....
—EDGAR ALLEN
POE

Date

Time

Date

Time

Date

_____

Time

_____

Date

Time

Date

Time

Dreams are
but interludes,
which fancy
makes...
—JOHN DRYDEN

Date

_____

Time

_____

Date

Time

Date

Time

Date

Time

I can never
decide whether
my dreams are
the result of my
thoughts, or my
thoughts the result
of my dreams.
It is very queer.
But my dreams
make conclusions
for me. They decide
things finally.
I dream a decision.
Sleep seems to
hammer out for
me the logical
conclusions of
my vague days,
and offer
me them
as dreams.

—D.H. Lawrence

Date

Time

Date

Time

Date

_____

Time

_____

Date

Time

One night I
dreamed I was a
butterfly,
fluttering hither
and thither,
content with
my lot.
Suddenly I
awoke and
I was
Chuang-tzu again.
Who am I
in reality?
A butterfly
dreaming that
I am Chuang-tzu
or Chuang-tzu
imagining he was
a butterfly?
—CHUANG-TZU

D a t e

T i m e

D a t e

T i m e

Date

Time

Date

Time

Yet it was but
a dream—
yet such
a dream...
—JOHN KEATS

D a t e

T i m e

Date

Time

Date
_____

Time
_____

Date

Time

I dream of you,
to wake: would
that I might /
Dream of you
and not wake
but slumber on...
—CHRISTINA
ROSSETTI

Date

Time

Date

Time

Date

_____

Time

_____

Date

Time

It seems to me
I am trying to tell
you a dream—
making a vain
attempt, because
no relation of a
dream can convey
the dream-
sensation, that
commingling of
absurdity, surprise,
and bewilderment
in a tremor of
struggling revolt,
that notion of
being captured
by the incredible
which is the
very essence
of dreams....

—JOSEPH CONRAD

Date

Time

Date

Time

Date

Time

Date

Time

Date

Time

Our memory
of dreams may
become lasting,
if they repeat
themselves
often enough.

—MARCEL PROUST

Date

Time

Date

Time

Date

Time

Date

Time

D a t e

_____

T i m e

_____

Dreams are the

touchstones of our

characters.

—HENRY DAVID
THOREAU

Date

Time

D a t e

T i m e

Date

Time

Date

Time

Date

_____

Time

_____

The dream is
not comparable
to the irregular
sounds of a
musical
instrument,
which, instead
of being touched
by the hand of
the musician, is
struck by some
outside force;
the dream is
not senseless,
not absurd....
—SIGMUND FREUD

Date

Time

Date

Time

Date

Time

Date

Time

Date

_____

Time

_____

That, if then I
had waked after a
long sleep,
Will make me
sleep again: and
then, in dreaming,
The clouds
methought would
open and
show riches
Ready to drop
upon me; that,
when I waked
I cried to
dream again.
—WILLIAM
SHAKESPEARE

Date

Time

Date

Time

Date

Time

When I placed
my head on my
pillow, I did not
sleep, nor could
I be said to think.
My imagination,
unbidden,
possessed and
guided me,
gifting the
successive images
that arose in my
mind with a
vividness far
beyond the
usual bounds
of reverie....
—MARY SHELLEY

Date

_____

Time

_____

Date

Time

Date

Time

Date

Time

D a t e

_____

T i m e

_____

If I were sitting
here describing a
dream...there'd
be a certain look
on your face.
And I know what
that look means
because I
feel it myself—
recognition.
The pleasure of
recognition, a bit
of rescue work,
so to speak,
rescuing the
formless
into form.
—DORIS LESSING

Date

Time

Date

_____

Time

_____

D a t e

T i m e

Date

Time

Date

_____

Time

_____

The man who
gets auspicious
dreams should
be looked upon
as a long-lived
man....

—SUSHRUTA,
600 B.C.

Date

Time

Date

Time

Date

_____

Time

_____

D a t e

_____

T i m e

_____

Dreamed a quite
formidably clear
dream of taking
a large front tooth
out, with part
of the jaw, and
looking to see
how much
disfigured I was,
in the glass,
saying at the
same time,
'Well, for once
this is no dream.'
—JOHN RUSKIN

Date
_____

Time
_____

D a t e

_____

T i m e

Date

_____

Time

_____

Date

Time

Date

Time

How does it
come about that
in this dream
I enjoy
indescribable
beauties of music
and in that one
soar and fly
upwards with the
delight of an eagle
to the most
distant heights?
—FRIEDRICH
NIETZSCHE

Date

Time

Date

Time

Date

Time

Date

Time

Date

Time

Traveler repose
and dream among
my leaves.
—WILLIAM BLAKE

Date

_____

Time

_____

Date

_____

Time

_____

Date

Time

DREAM DICTIONARY

Following is a list of common dream symbols and their possible meanings. These symbols do not have concrete explanations or definitions; it's important to explore *your* associations with the symbols to help you better understand what they could mean to you. In his book, *Dreams That Can Change Your Life,* psychologist Alan B. Siegel sums it up: "A useful approach is to view dream work as a journey of discovery on which we encounter many ideas, theories, and hunches that make our dream more meaningful and our feelings more understandable. Keep in mind that enjoying the journey can be as important as arriving at its endpoint."

With this in mind, the following is a sampling of interpretations of some common dream symbols. They are culled from Sigmund Freud's *The Interpretation of Dreams;* Carl Jung's *Memories, Dreams, and Reflections;* and Eric Ackroyd's *A Dictionary of Dream Symbols.* (See suggested reading for more information on these books.)

AIRPLANE: Two common interpretations exist here: Freud would call it a sexual symbol, describing its forceful motion as reminiscent of a penis. It can also symbolize liberation or freedom. A glider or bird could also represent this second interpretation.

ANGEL: Angels often represent the conscience; a part of you issuing a warning or giving a blessing of something.

BABY: In non-pregnant women, a baby can symbolize your innocent self, or vulnerability. It also may represent the desire for a child.

BAT: If you are frightened of these night birds, a bat may represent something dark or repressed in your life.

BLUE: Depending on your associations, blue can represent masculinity (unless it's the ocean, which may represent the feminine). If it is dark, blue can symbolize depression or the unconscious (see Darkness).

CAGE: Most commonly, this represents a restriction in your life, something you're hiding or a desire for freedom.

CAR: Cars often represent yourself and, depending on how you're driving, how you feel about the direction of your life. Freud would label this a phallic symbol.

CATS: Here it's important to think of your own associations with cats. In general, however, they are thought to represent femininity: your own femininity or a woman in your life.

DREAM DICTIONARY, CONT.

DARKNESS: Darkness or nighttime is often considered to represent the unconscious. This can be seen as fear of your unconscious or an invitation to explore it.

DOG: Dogs can represent a variety of things depending on your associations with them. Often they're linked to the animal nature of yourself or someone close to you.

EARTH: The earth in a dream can mean a number of things. It is often a symbol of femininity or your mother ("mother earth"). On the other hand, it sometimes represents one's self or one's feelings for one's life.

EATING: Eating generally represents self-gratification in some area of your life: work, relationships, etc.

EYE: The eye usually has a connotation of wisdom or seeking wisdom. It can also represent the self in its search for wisdom.

FISH: Fish often are thought to represent fertility; Jung considered them to represent the unconscious (see Darkness). Fishing can represent delving into the unconscious.

HAIR: Hair sometimes symbolizes virility or sexuality. A loss of hair could represent being threatened along these lines. If the hair is white, it could refer to wisdom.

HOUSE: A house may represent the self, your life, or family. The shape or condition of the house may symbolize how you feel about yourself. Going "upstairs" is thought to represent the head. If the house is where you grew up, it may be related to your feelings about your childhood and parents.

JUDGE: A judge, like an eye, may represent wisdom, or your conscience. It may even represent moral conscience or morality being imposed on you.

MONSTER: Like darkness, monsters usually represent your unconscious: your fear of wrestling with your deeper self.

OVEN: Ovens are sometimes thought to represent the womb, pregnancy, or a desire for pregnancy. Freud would label it and any other opening or vessel a symbol of the vagina.

POOL: A pool or lake may refer to the self or self-reflection.

RED: It is important to think of your feelings about this color, but in general, it represents power, passion, or anger.

RIVER: Rivers themselves are thought to represent sexuality or vitality, while crossing a river may refer to a significant change in one's life or thoughts.

DREAM DICTIONARY, CONT.

ROCK: Rocks usually symbolize steadfastness and patience. Depending on the dream, they may also represent a danger or threat.

SHIP: Ships and the ocean are generally thought to be feminine symbols, representing your femininity, your mother, or a woman in your life.

SNAKE: Depending on your associations, a snake can be a phallic symbol or, in the Christian tradition, a symbol of evil. A shedding snake may represent rejuvenation in your life.

STAIRS: Stairs may mean a change in your life, moving to a different plane, etc. According to Freud, stairs refer to sexual intercourse.

SUN: The sun may represent the self, or sometimes a father figure. It also may connote enlightenment or progress.

TEETH: Depending on the dream, teeth may represent fear of violence (biting) or aggressiveness. Losing teeth may symbolize life: a return to infancy or fear of mortality.

TREE: A tree or garden may represent life and growth. The state of the tree may give a clue as to how you feel about yourself and your life direction.

TUNNEL: Freud said a tunnel represents the vagina; a train or car entering it represents intercourse. While this is the most popular meaning, it also may represent the unconscious.

VOLCANO: Volcanoes or explosions are often signs of something erupting within you; possibly something sexual or emotional. It may represent relieving something repressed.

WATER: Depending on the dream, water can have a wide variety of connotations. It may represent the feminine (your mother or a woman in your life), or some life force or energy. Deep water may represent the unconscious, or possibly fear. Rushing water can mean growth or creativity.

WIND: The wind can symbolize a change or need for change in one's life, or wild, unsettled emotions.

ZODIAC SIGN: Your zodiac sign in a dream may symbolize the self or your life path. It may also represent the parts of yourself that are unknown, or unconscious.

PERSONAL SYMBOLS LOG

In the following pages, you can describe or sketch examples of any symbols that occur in your dreams.

PERSONAL SYMBOLS LOG

PERSONAL SYMBOLS LOG

PERSONAL SYMBOLS LOG

PERSONAL SYMBOLS LOG

PERSONAL SYMBOLS LOG

RECURRING THEMES LOG

RECURRING THEMES LOG

RECURRING THEMES LOG

RECURRING THEMES LOG

RECURRING THEMES LOG

SUGGESTED READING

ERIC ACKROYD *A Dictionary of Dream Symbols*, A Blandford Book, 1993. A comprehensive guide containing over 700 dream symbols and their possible interpretations.

ROBERT BOSNAK *A Little Course in Dreams: A Basic Handbook of Jungian Dreamwork*, Shambhala, 1993. A pocket-sized guide to dream meaning and interpretation, featuring lessons and exercises.

STEPHEN BROOK, ED. *The Oxford Book of Dreams*, Oxford University Press, 1983. A comprehensive literary anthology of dreams and dreaming, from Plato to Poe.

CARLOS CASTENEDA *The Art of Dreaming*, HarperCollins, 1993. After six years, the author of the Don Juan books breaks his silence with an in-depth study of dreams and their meanings.

DAVID FONTANA *The Secret Language of Dreams*, Chronicle, 1994. Beautifully illustrated and expertly written, *The Secret Language of Dreams* explores the oddities and ambiguities of our sleeping world.

SIGMUND FREUD *The Interpretation of Dreams*, MacMillan 1913; rereleased Avon, 1965. Freud originated psychoanalysis, a treatment centered around the discovery of emotional life episodes, usually through dream interpretation,

ANA LORA GARRARD *An Invitation to Dream: Tapping the Resources of Inner Wisdom*, Llewellyn Publications, 1993. A dream workbook that shuns dictionary interpretations in favor of personal writing, meditation, and artwork.

CARL GUSTAV JUNG *Memories, Dreams, and Reflections*, Pantheon, 1963, rereleased Vintage, 1989. Jung also used dream interpretation in his therapy, but differed from Freud in that he stressed the collective unconscious—the idea that all dreamers share timeless elements of human experience. These ideas are detailed in this autobiography.

GUSTAV HINDMAN MILLER *10,000 Dreams Interpreted*, Barnes and Noble, 1992. This classic encyclopedia of dream interpretation, written around the turn of the century, has just been rereleased in a replica of the original edition.

ALAN B. SIEGEL, PH.D. *Dreams That Can Change Your Life*, Jeremy Tarcher, 1990. How to learn from your "turning point" dreams—those dreams in times of heightened pressure that carry special meaning.